BAIKAL
SACRED SEA OF SIBERIA

ESSAY BY PETER MATTHIESSEN
PHOTOGRAPHS BY BOYD NORTON
FOREWORD BY YEVGENY YEVTUSHENKO
AFTERWORD BY DAVID BROWER

Edited by Chez Liley

SIERRA CLUB BOOKS

San Francisco

Library of Congress Cataloging-in-Publication Data

Matthiessen, Peter.
    Baikal : sacred sea of Siberia / essay by Peter Matthiessen : photographs by Boyd Norton.
        p.   cm.
    ISBN 0-87156-584-6
    I. Baikal Lake (R.S.F.S.R.)—Description and travel.
    2. Matthiessen, Peter—Journeys—Russian S.F.S.R.—Baikal Lake. I. Norton, Boyd.   II. Title.
DK771.B3M386   1992
915.7′5—dc20   92-3057
                                                                  CIP

PRODUCTION Susan Ristow
COMPOSITION Wilsted & Taylor

Printed by Dai Nippon Printing Co. (Hong Kong) Ltd.

10 9 8 7 6 5 4 3 2 1

For Paul Winter and Chez Liley
and all our excellent friends
on board the *Baikal*

CONTENTS

"The sacred sea," "the sacred lake," "the sacred water"—that is what native inhabitants have called Baikal from the beginning of time. So have Russians, who had already arrived on its shores by the seventeenth century, as well as travelers from abroad, admiring its majestic, supernatural mystery and beauty. The reverence for Baikal held by uncivilized people and also by those considered enlightened for their time was equally complete and captivating, even though it touched mainly the mystical feelings in the one and the aesthetic and scientific impulses in the other. The sight of Baikal would dumbfound them every time because it did not fit their conceptions either of spirit or of matter. Baikal was located where something like that should have been impossible, it was not the sort of thing that should have been possible here or anywhere else, and it did not have the same effect on the soul that "indifferent" nature usually does. This was something uncommon, special, and "wrought by God."

Baikal was measured and studied in due course, even, in recent years, with the aid of deep-sea instruments. It acquired definite dimensions and became subject to comparison, alternately likened to Lake Tanganyika and to the Caspian Sea. They've calculated that it holds one fifth of all fresh water on our planet, they've explained its origin, and they've conjectured as to how species of plants, animals, and fish existing nowhere else could originate here and how species found only in other parts of the world many thousands of miles away managed to end up here. Not all these explanations and conjectures tally even with each other. Baikal is not so simple that it could be deprived of its mystery and enigma that easily, but based on its physical properties it has, nevertheless, been assigned a fitting place alongside other great wonders that have already been discovered and described, as well it should. And it stands alongside them solely because Baikal itself, alive, majestic, and not created by human hands, not comparable to anything and not repeated anywhere, is aware of its own primordial place and its own life force.

VALENTIN RASPUTIN from "Baikal"

A gnarled pine on the flanks of Maloye Kolokolnik ("Small Bell Tower") above the shore of Peschanaya Bay, Pribaikalsky National Park, west shore.

ix

FOREWORD

I WAS BORN in Siberia about three hundred kilometers from Lake Baikal in a railroad junction town with the cold name of Zima (winter). At that time I could not have envisioned that one day I would have an American friend whose name was the same as my native town: Winter.*

At the end of the nineteenth century my Ukrainian peasant ancestors were exiled here for setting fire to the estate manor house. With a blow of her fist, according to family legend, my great-grandmother killed a gendarme of the Tsar who had been sent to put down the rebellion. My ancestors walked the more than eleven thousand kilometers to Siberia with chains on their legs that pounded them bloody. At that time the principal music of Siberia was the clanging of chains. The most famous song of Siberia was about an escaped convict who climbed into a salty-fish barrel, made a sail of his tattered shirt, and endeavored to cross Baikal, beautiful in its majesty and terrifying in its fury. But if escape was possible from pre-revolutionary Siberian penal servitude, it became almost impossible when the socialist dictatorship enclosed the beauty of Siberian nature with the barbed wire of the gulag and threw millions of people behind it. Every spring, when the snow began to melt in the Siberian taiga, corpses of

Toward your crags,
  Baikal,
unafraid of hurting myself on crags,
I was forever rowing—
a fugitive convict of fame.
Without you the horizon
in Russia could not be radiant.
If you are polluted,
I cannot feel myself clean.
Like a cry of purity
resounding
  over the perishing blue
comes your voice:
  "Protect me,
protect me,
  do you hear, my Son?!"

     from *Baikal*

---

* Yevgeny Yevtushenko met the musician Paul Winter in 1984, and inspired him to visit Baikal. Winter's seventh trip to the Soviet Union, in 1990, accompanied by Peter Matthiessen on an expedition around Lake Baikal, sowed the seed for this book.

View from a cliff in Pribaikalsky National Park, high above Aya Bay.

xi

people who had attempted to escape began to show through. With bitterness they were called "snow-drops," like the first spring flowers. For those exiled or imprisoned, the word "Siberia" became a symbol of non-freedom and violence. But still, people would sing this spirited folk song:

And what is Siberia? I don't fear Siberia.

Siberia is also the Russian land.

And this was also true, because for those who were born in Siberia, the word was at the same time a symbol of wild, untamed beauty and rigorously tender nature.

Baikal is the blue heart of Siberia. It pulses amidst the green ocean of the taiga, rocking in its depths the ghosts of escaped convicts; on its bottom, overgrown with seaweed, lie their sawed shackles that one day, with a triumphant howl of joy, had been thrown in the water. Along the shores of Baikal stand tiny hunters' huts, belonging to no one and at the same time to everyone, where, by custom, each visitor leaves behind for the next some cartridges, matches, and salt. Here already are other laws—not governmental, but Siberian—where there reigns not bureaucracy but a feeling of common danger in the face of threatening elements that might appear suddenly like a wounded bear, or the scorching white face of frost which can transform into a statue of ice anyone who submits to exhaustion and lies down in a snowdrift. Siberians are children of a gigantic space so wearied by non-freedom that it has become a materialized yearning for freedom, a longing that is splashed across many thousands of kilometers—the roaring longing of rivers, of murmuring green summits of the taiga, of snarling bears.

People of the so-called capitalist and socialist worlds have come face to face with the same tragedy—the deficiency of freedom. In capitalism this deficiency is less apparent because it is masked by the illusion of freedom, while that which was called socialism has collapsed just because of the degrading visibility of this deficiency. Absolute freedom isn't possible—indeed, it would be criminal, for a man who has become completely free becomes free from his conscience and from a sense of beauty, and that is fascism. But there is a grand sense of freedom preserved in feeling the preciousness of space, in feeling the uniqueness of each blade of grass on which the dew gleams like tiny eyes of the earth. Precisely because we die with rapture before the wide-open lap of the Grand Canyon, and before Baikal, which seethes in anger and caressingly licks its shores in moments of tenderness, we are in this instant neither Russian nor American, but heirs of the indivisible treasury of all humankind: nature.

Dostoyevsky once formulated the prophetic term "omniresponse." This is what is needed now most of all in art and politics. To be a patriot only of one's own country is insufficient, even criminal, because one national egoism unavoidably comes into conflict with another. Patriotism of all humanity is the only salvation. People like Peter Matthiessen, Paul Winter, and Boyd Norton are—thank God!—removed from politics, but all three belong to a profession I call "rescuers," gathering together, kernel by kernel, dewdrop by dewdrop, crumb by crumb, all the beauty scattered over the earth. They have succeeded in lifting Lake Baikal in their arms like a gigantic silver disc and drawing it near to the Grand Canyon, their country's equivalent symbol of natural wonder, so that through nature they might come to know each other and become brothers forever, as did Paul Winter, born in Altoona, Pennsylvania, and I, born in Zima Junction, Siberia. Once, when I was limping after an operation, Paul Winter gave me a family relic—his father's apple-tree walking stick. Although it is dried out and many years old, it sometimes seems to me that if I would thrust it into Russian earth, this stick would begin to blossom and be covered with apples. In essence, Paul Winter's father's stick bore fruit long ago, one of which is this book. If all people on earth were so universally human as Peter Matthiessen, Paul Winter, and Boyd Norton, there would be no more wars. Dostoyevsky once wrote: "Beauty will save the world."

But who will save beauty?

YEVGENY YEVTUSHENKO
29 January 1992, New York
(*Translated by Albert C. Todd*)

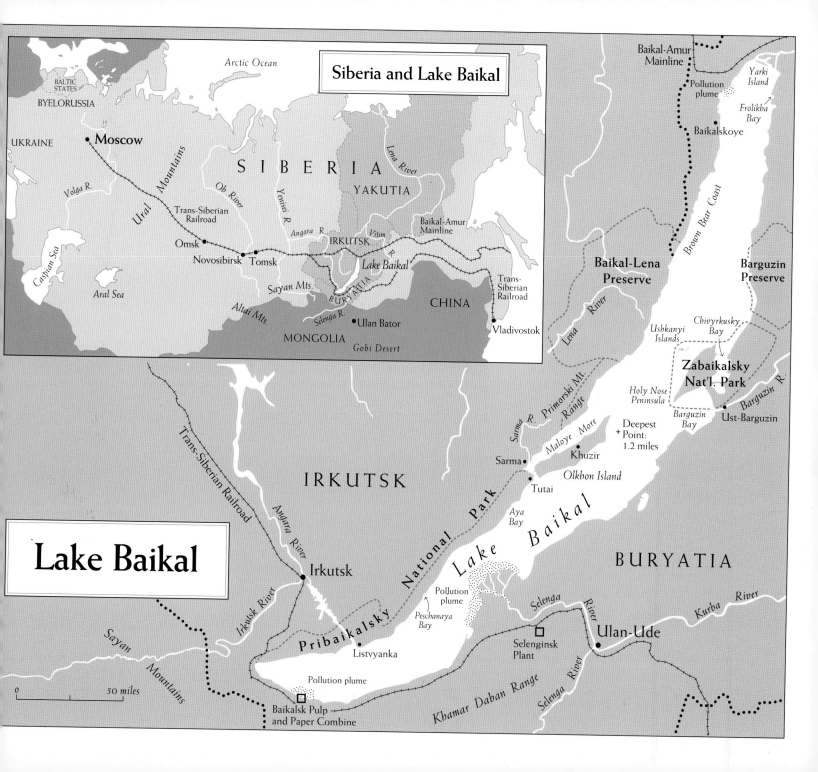

Lake Baikal

Siberia and Lake Baikal

Arctic Ocean

BALTIC
STATES
BYELORUSSIA
UKRAINE
Moscow

Volga R.
Ural Mountains
Caspian Sea
Aral Sea

S I B E R I A

Ob River
Yenisei R.
Angara R.
Omsk
Novosibirsk   Tomsk
Sayan Mts.
Altai Mts.
Selenga R.
MONGOLIA   Ulan Bator
Gobi Desert

Lena River
YAKUTIA

Baikal-Amur
Mainline
Vitim
IRKUTSK   R.
Lake Baikal
BURYATIA
CHINA

Trans-
Siberian
Railroad
Vladivostok

Trans-Siberian
Railroad

Baikal-Amur
Mainline
Pollution
plume
Yarki
Island
Frolikha
Bay
Baikalskoye

Brown Bear Coast

Baikal-Lena
Preserve

Barguzin
Preserve

Lena   River

Lena   River

Ushkanyi
Islands
Chivyrkusky
Bay

Zabaikalsky
Nat'l. Park

Holy Nose
Peninsula
Barguzin
Bay
Ust-Barguzin
Barguzin R.

Trans-Siberian Railroad

Angara River

IRKUTSK

Irkutsk

Irkutsk River

Sayan
Mountains

0   50 miles

Pribaikalsky

National Park

Sarma R.
Primorski Mt.
Range

Deepest
+ Point:
1.2 miles

Sarma
Tutai
Maloye More
Khuzir
Olkhon Island

Aya
Bay

Lake   Baikal

BURYATIA

Pollution
plume
Peschanaya
Bay

Selenga
Selenga   River
Selenginsk
Plant

Listvyanka

Pollution plume

Baikalsk Pulp
and Paper Combine

Khamar Daban Range

Selenga   River

Kurba   River

Ulan-Ude

PART ONE

High hills and exceedingly high rocky cliffs are all around it—over twenty times one thousand versts and more have I dragged myself and nowhere seen any like unto these. . . . Exceedingly many birds, geese, and swans swim upon the sea covering it like snow. It hath fishes—sturgeon, and salmon, sterlet, and omul, and whitefish, and many other kinds.
The water is fresh and hath great seals and sea lions in it: when I dwelt in Mezen, I saw nought like unto these in the big sea. And the fishes there are plentiful: the sturgeon and salmon are surpassingly fat—thou canst not fry them in a pan, for there will be nought but grease. And all this hath been wrought by Christ in heaven for mankind so that, resting content, he shouldst render praise unto God.

—Archpriest Avvakum, 1662

PART ONE

P AST EIGHT in the evening on the last day of August, after a ten-hour climb, we haul ourselves to the high rim of the Baikal Canyon. From where we stand, high plateaus, in hard, clear light, seem to stretch forever westward to the Urals. Facing east, my companion, the huge Siberian woodsman Semyon Ustinov, spreads his long arms. Far below, his beloved Baikal, the most ancient lake on earth, is shrouded in mist that drifts up the steep talus slope as if in search of us. The canyon rim on which we stand is a mile or more above the surface of the lake, whose greatest depth is 5,750 feet, or 1.1 miles, with an additional four miles of sediment above the bedrock. The great Baikal rift is seven times as deep as the Grand Canyon, by far the deepest land depression on the planet.

For the past week we have been exploring Lake Baikal and talking about the threats to its ecology with a group including Semyon and his friend the controversial writer Valentin Rasputin. The lake, which lies in a great crescent nearly 400 miles long, fills a widening valley where two tectonic plates, pulling apart, drop the depression ever lower. This vast plateau north and west of Baikal, known to geologists as the Siberian Platform, is being separated from Asia to the south and east by this shift in the earth's crust. Because the fault's floor is widening about one inch every year, Baikal can collect new sediment

3

I arrived on the 1st of February at the Fort *Buratz:* which place, and all along to the Lake *Baikal,* is watered by the River *Angara,* and inhabited by the *Burattians.* . . . If they are obliged to the taking of any Oath amongst themselves, they go to the Lake *Baikal,* near which is a Hill that they esteem Sacred, to which they can ride in two Days. Upon this high Mountain they take their Oath, and firmly believe the false Swearer shall never come down alive. To this Hill they frequently offer up all sorts of slaughtered Cattle, and have paid a veneration to it for many Years. . . . The Water of the Lake tasts [sic] very fresh, is clear, and of a deep Green, like that of the Ocean. Where the Ice was open we often observed a great many Sea-Dogs, who were all blackish, and not variegated, like those in the White Sea. Here are also great multitudes of Fish, as large *Sturgeons* and *Jacks,* of which I have seen some that weighed two hundred *German* Pounds. . . . It was very zealously warned and entreated by several Persons, that when I came upon this dangerous Water, I should not call it a still *Water* or *Lake,* but a *Sea;* they alledging [sic] that formerly several considerable Persons, who had been on this *Sea,* and ventured to call it . . . *Standing Water,* were immediately overtaken by violently Stormy Winds, and were in great danger of their Lives. . . . (His Excellency E. Ysbrants Ides, *Three Years Travel from Moscovy Over Land to China,* 1706)

The Barguzin Valley and River, east of Baikal.

without any loss to its huge volume of water. Although its surface is more or less the size of Lake Superior, Baikal holds nearly the equivalent of all five of the Great Lakes, or about one-fifth of all the fresh water on earth. (This astonishing volume might be better understood another way: if all of Baikal's 334 tributaries were diverted, and its sole outlet, the Angara River, were to drain it, the emptying would take four hundred years. The Amazon, Ganges, Mississippi, Nile, and Congo, together with all the other rivers and streams on earth, would have to flow a year or more just to refill it.)

Because the rift grows ever larger, the four miles of lake floor contain matter that has accumulated for twenty to thirty million years. (Lake Tanganyika, in Africa's Western Rift Valley, which looks like a miniature Baikal even in its distinctive crescent shape, is the earth's second oldest lake—2,000,000 years—and second deepest, at 4,700 feet.) Even the largest of ordinary lakes may live at most 50,000 years before they fill with silt, evaporate, and die, and, by this criterion, "The Blue Pearl of Siberia" is all but eternal. It is often called an inland sea—"Ye glorious sea, ye sacred Baikal" goes an old Siberian song—or even, like the Red Sea, an incipient ocean. Hydrothermal vents in the lake floor at Frolikha Bay, in the northeast—the first such vents ever located in fresh water—support rich communities of bottom life, including translucent shrimps and snails, large mushroom-shaped sponges, and other forms ordinarily associated with salt water. What is more, life exists right to the bottom (in Lake Tanganyika it dies out a few hundred feet down) because of deep oxygen circulation that is thought to be caused by mysterious tides drawn from such deep water by the sun and moon.

Warm water from vents in the cold deeps doubtless contributes to the plenitude of life. Whereas an ordinary lake might have three am-

phipod species and eight flatworms, Baikal has 255 amphipods and 80 flatworms, including a brute well over a foot long that devours fish. Of Baikal's 2,000-odd aquatic forms, at least 1,200 are endemic; two-thirds of the lake's flora and much of its fauna are found nowhere else. Among these is the nerpa, the only fresh water seal on earth, a creature I have long wanted to see.

Little sediment enters Baikal from the crystalline rock formations all around, which release a bare trace of salts and other minerals; the primordial deep, left undisturbed, is traditionally as clear and pure as distilled water. Its extreme clarity is intensified by the activities of a minute crustacean, *Baikal epishura,* which strains out algaes, plankton, and bacteria. In good years, the 3,000,000 epishura that inhabit the water column under each square meter of the surface keep the water so pristine that a bright kopeck, cast away, might still be seen glinting a hundred feet below.

Epishura is but one of the hundreds of endemic crustaceans, including 200-odd species of freshwater shrimp, that make the lake a vast laboratory for the study of ecology and evolution. For all these reasons, this huge blue crescent in the farthest part of Central Asia is generally considered the most interesting body of water on the earth.

Like the Galapagos, Baikal is a closed ecosystem, since all of the lake's water comes from these surrounding mountains, and the whole watershed is only twice as large as the lake itself. Even its main tributary, the Selenga River, which brings about half of Baikal's water north out of Mongolia, is entirely isolated from other watersheds or river systems and introduces no outside genetic influence. The forests surrounding Lake Baikal have few endemic species, yet they abound in robust Siberian wildlife, including the lustrous tree weasel called the sable, as well as red and musk deer, moose, Eurasian wolves, brown bears, and, not so many years ago, the Siberian tiger. One also

Spring breakup of ice on Maloye Morye, west shore. (Photo: Boris Dmitriev)

7

finds the turkey-sized wildfowl called the capercaille, a huge black grouse which is rumored to become so transported by its own courtship song that it closes its eyes and deafens itself with its own din.

Semyon Ustinov was born east of the lake at a village called Fox Place, in the country of the Buryat Mongol people north of Ulan Ude, and he speaks movingly of the River Kurba, where he spent many lonely hours as a boy. One day near sunset, from a large hill across the stream, he heard a Buryat shepherdess on horseback "singing about everything she saw, and her singing harmonized heaven, earth, and mountains." He remembers "the currents of water filled with light, and how her high voice, singing of them, was so pure and clear." Some years later his father took him to the high point in the eastern mountains from where the boy first saw the sacred lake. "I understood at once," he says, "that Baikal represented the same mysterious totality of the universe that the Buryat shepherdess was celebrating in her song."

Here on the peak of the Baikal ridge the wind is growing cold. A lone raptor, as if drawn to the last sunlight, circles high in a darkening blue sky that will fill with stars. Quickly, in dusk, we descend loose rocks to a small gorge with a rivulet of cold gray water. Dark comes as the last dry wood is gathered from silver skeletons of a recumbent pine. We build our fire and make tea, devouring dry hunks of bread and sausage. Already the half moon has gone behind a sharp peak of the rim, and with no light on this treacherous incline, we must perch all night on big, cold, broken slabs, huddled close to the wind-whipped fire, one side burning and the other freezing in temperatures which, by Semyon's estimate, would fall into the thirties before dawn.

During a long night spent thinly clad on rocks on a steep mountainside, I have time to consider why I find myself in such hard cir-

The Barguzin Range rises abruptly from the valley floor to an elevation of approximately 7,500 feet.

8

cumstances after scarcely a fortnight in the Soviet Union. The reason lies below, in great Baikal, which has drawn me since the day, long years ago, that I first learned of a primordial deep lake of diamantine clarity that lay off to the north of the Gobi Desert. Even today, despite serious damage, Baikal remains the cleanest large lake in the world, not because care has been taken but because its enormous depth and volume have absorbed—so far—man's efforts to despoil it. Only recently has it been known how swiftly the lake's ancient ecology could unravel, and how close man has come to losing it forever.

The decline began less than a century ago with the arrival in 1896 of the Trans-Siberian Railway, which rounds the south end of the lake on its way east. Crude timbering and primitive agriculture soon followed, bringing erosion and increasing silt into the lake, but no fatal destruction was threatened until 1957, when a vast industry at the lake's south end was approved by the state planning boards in Moscow. The Baikalsk Pulp and Paper Combine would exploit the limitless timber and pristine water required to produce cellulose for the manufacture of high-quality rayon cord used in airplane tires.

Construction was about to begin when, in 1961, Dr. Grigory Galazii, director of the Limnological Institute of the USSR Academy of Sciences at nearby Irkutsk, warned that the cellulose plant together with a smaller combine in the Selenga River would do permanent damage to the lake's ecological balance. Alarmed articles soon set in motion an organized defense of the sacred lake that most citizens would never see, yet which was to become the emblem and first battleground of the USSR's environmental struggle. (In the same period the Siberian writer Sergei Zalygin, now the editor of *Novy Mir*, spoke out against the planned construction of a hydroelectric dam on the Ob River that would have flooded an enormous tract to the northwest. The Soviet environmental movement had begun.) In 1963, Mi-

Village on the west shore.
(Photo: Ben Simmons)

11

The surface of Lake Baikál is more than 400 feet higher than the city of Irkútsk, and the river Angará, through which the lake discharges into the arctic ocean [sic], falls that 400 feet in a distance of 40 miles, making a current that is everywhere extremely swift, and that runs in some places at the rate of 12 or 15 miles an hour. Steamers ply back and forth between the city and the lake, but they are six or eight hours in struggling up-stream, while they come down in about two. At the outlet, where the current is swiftest, the river never entirely freezes over, and it does not close opposite Irkútsk until some time in January, although the thermometer frequently goes to forty degrees below zero in December. The Angará is in all respects a peculiar and original river. Instead of coming into existence as a brook, it is born a mile wide with a current like a mill-race. Although its water, even in the hottest midsummer weather, is icy cold, it is the very last river in Siberia to freeze. It chills the adventurous bather to the bone in August, and then in the coldest weather of December steams as if it were boiling. Finally, it overflows its banks, not in the spring, when other rivers overflow theirs, but in early winter, when all other streams are locked in ice. (George Kennan, *The Siberian Exile System*, 1970)

In the village of Ust Barguzin, east shore of Baikal.

khail Sholokhov, the author of *And Quiet Flows the Don,* denounced the pulp mills at the Communist Party Congress; there was also a supporting letter from Siberia's intellectuals.

Claiming that the rayon cord was needed by the Air Force, the bureaucrats of the USSR State Planning Committee denounced these early champions of the environment as CIA agents and traitors. The Siberians' protests were entirely unavailing, and the Baikalsk plant began operation in 1966, despite general agreement that it could have been built downstream from the lake on the already polluted Angara River, at 35 to 40 percent less cost, and that, anyway, a better, cheaper, tire cord of lighter weight made from metal and synthetic fibers was already available. A series of subsequent experiments with effluent control failed to keep toxic chemicals out of the lake, and meanwhile the clearing of large stands of timber devastated much of the surrounding taiga, or boreal forest, causing increased erosion and siltation. There was also serious contamination from factory wastes and untreated sewage dumped into the Selenga River at Ulan Ude, made worse by the strong chemicals from the Selenginsk pulp factory downriver. In 1968, the Irkutsk soviet forbade environmentally destructive enterprises in this province, but its rulings were systematically ignored.

Earlier, in the 1950s, construction of the first hydroelectric dam on the Angara had begun at Irkutsk, followed by an immense dam at Bratsk. The four dams currently in operation have brought a welter of heavy industry to the four cities in the once-beautiful Angara Valley, which is now as polluted as any region in European Russia. Meanwhile, the old river villages disappeared beneath the flood.

Paul Winter first came to Lake Baikal in 1984 on his second trip to the

Soviet Union. Stirred by Baikal's beauty and immensity, Winter returned twice in the next year with the idea of composing a "Baikal Suite" that might help to convey not only the wonder of Russia's sacred lake, but also its urgent symbolism in the worldwide rise of environmental consciousness. The suite would be based on the mythic adventures of a young Russian boy, and the music would be counterpointed by the sounds of nature—water, wind, and echo—as well as the voices of wild creatures, an effect he had already experimented with successfully in musical colloquies with wolves, elephants, and whales.

In September 1986, during a concert tour of the USSR, his ensemble, the Paul Winter Consort, was finally permitted a brief boat excursion on the lake, which has been generally inaccessible to Russians and all but forbidden to foreigners. By this time Winter was acquainted with Dr. Grigory Galazii of the Limnological Institute, who for nearly three decades, until he was removed in the mid-eighties, refuted the self-serving data produced by the "scientists" at the Baikalsk pulp plant and issued stubborn warnings of a future crisis. The poet Yevgeny Yevtushenko introduced Winter to the Siberian writer, environmentalist, and later a member of the Politburo, Valentin Rasputin, and it was Rasputin who guided him on an extensive survey of the lake in 1988. They were accompanied by Semyon Ustinov, who has lived at Baikal since 1952 and spends most of the year in this remote region where we now find ourselves—the Brown Bear Coast, sixty-six miles along Baikal's northwest shore, which was set aside in 1988 as the Baikal–Lena Nature Preserve, with Ustinov as deputy director.

Beginning with the album *Common Ground* (1979), Paul Winter, an imaginative jazz musician, has turned increasingly to nature for his inspiration, and his generosity in the environmental cause has made

Clay figures, Ust Barguzin.
(Photo: Ben Simmons)

In the fishing village of Baikalskoye on the northwest shore.

15

him a favorite of the Russians. In the same spirit Winter telephoned me in July 1990 to invite me along that summer on his Baikal expedition, although he had never met me in his life. There were no conditions on the invitation, yet he felt confident that Baikal itself would induce me to write something in its defense, and indeed I kept a diary as we traveled.

Paul Winter with Russian and Japanese collaborators on Big Ushkanyi Island, working on a film documentary about Lake Baikal. (Photo: Ben Simmons)

PART TWO

In our speech it means fiery place, here formerly was solid fire, then the land collapsed and it became a sea. From that time we call our sea Baigal.

—L. E. Eliasov, *From Where Does The Name "Baikal" Come?*

PART TWO

August 21.

W E MEET in the Domodeveo air terminal east of Moscow, and
depart together for Irkutsk, the capital of Siberia, a journey
approximately as long as the journey from New York to Moscow. The
plane crosses the Urals after midnight, not far north of the town of
Nizhni Tagil, on the eastern slope, where air pollution is so intense,
according to one factory worker, that "at our works, pigeons disappeared long ago. We don't even have crows. We look up at the sky and
we are horrified."[1]

To the south lies the Caspian Sea, afflicted these days with high
counts of dangerous chemicals known as phenols, and farther east,
what is left of the great Aral Sea, which, because of unwise and heavy-
handed irrigation projects commenced at the same time as the
exploration of Baikal, has shrunk by two-thirds in the past twenty-
eight years.

East of Omsk and west of Tomsk, the plane descends through dark,
foul weather to lone lights sadly separated from one another, like the
mast lights of scattered fishing vessels moored in darkness. This is Novosibirsk (New Siberia), the most populous Siberian city. All around
is the black and hulking taiga, mostly evergreen, that comprises more
of the land surface of the USSR than the steppes and deserts, the
mountains, seas, tilled lands, and tundra all together.

Before daylight we are aloft again, headed east across the River Ob
into the dawn. The rain has stopped and a glow appears over the wing,

Bay of Aya, west bank of Baikal, Irkutsk province.
(Photo: Susie Crate)

Rhododendron blossoms in May, Peschanaya Bay.

21

In 1631 the ataman (headman) Perfilyeff built the first fort called "Bratski", in the Buriat territory; in 1646 the ataman Kolesnikoff reached the Angara and built a small fort at the mouth of the r. Ossa; in 1654 the fort Balaganski and in 1661 the fort Irkutski were built. Almost simultaneously with this move another one beyond the Baikal was started by the Russians from Yakutsk which had come into existance [sic] in 1632 and had soon become a separate "voyevodstvo" (district governed by a "voyevoda"—military governor). In 1641 the Verkholenski fort was built; in 1643 the Russians reached the Baikal and occupied the island Olhon; in 1648 the son of a boyar (noble), Galkin, reached the mouth of the r. Barguzin and there built the fort Barguzinski which became the *point d'appui* of the Russians in Transbaikalia. (V. A. Ryazanovski, *Customary Law of the Mongol Tribes,* 1929)

Taiga, mixed forest of birch, larch, and pine, southeast shore of Baikal.

and earth and sky separate at last as daybreak illumines a great formless swamp and a wide river. This is the beautiful Angara, which flows out of the southwest end of Lake Baikal. The sun appears as the plane circles Irkutsk.

Sib Ir (the "Sleeping Land" of the native Buryat Mongols who ruled the region when the first Cossacks arrived in the seventeenth century) is still widely discounted as a dark and barbarous land of icy cold, wind, trackless swamp, and labyrinthine forest, of starving wild beasts and desperate prisoners. But the Siberian capital of Irkutsk, at one time (like St. Louis) a frontier trading station about two-thirds of the way between the Urals and the Pacific, arose at the crossing of many ancient routes to Mongolia, Tibet, and China, and could already claim a geographic institute at the time of American independence. Irkutsk equipped Russia's expeditions to the Pacific, including those which discovered the Bering Sea and founded the first European settlements in Alaska and northern California.

In the southeast, forty miles away, there billows from beneath the lake horizon a heavy shroud of yellowish smoke that thickens the clouds as it blows east over the forests. Thanks to Lake Baikal's defenders, it has been decided that the Baikalsk plant will turn to making furniture by 1993, but meanwhile the dumping of its chemically contaminated waste water will continue, although it has already ruined twenty-three square miles of the lake's floor. This latter figure represents the area of dead lake bottom; more insidious pollution has spread so far northward that the Intourist hotel here at the lakeshore fishing village of Listvyanka can no longer serve the celebrated water straight from the lake. (In recent years, a state ministry plan to pipe Baikalsk's toxic waste across country to the Irkut River was fought by Grigory Galazii, Valentin Rasputin, and many others.)

Air pollution from that yellow cloud does even more harm than the

dumping of waste water. At latest estimate, the toxic fallout has damaged perhaps 770 square miles of taiga, in particular the fir trees, and this local situation is made worse by pollution from other sources. Wind-borne sulphur and nitrogen oxides from coal-burning industries on the Angara River to the west pour acid rain into the lake, and analysis of the lake sediments shows that polluting chemicals used in plastic manufacture have come on the winds from European Russia, thousands of miles away. Contamination resulting from poor agricultural practice on the southeast shore, together with erosion from overgrazed lands, does further damage, as does logging silt and log detritus in the streams. Oil tankers crisscross a lake with violent and eerily erratic weather (notably the sudden *Sarma* wind that bursts from the Sarma River valley on the northwest shore, with gusts of up to ninety miles an hour), and rickety oil tanks have been set up in an earthquake zone that in 1861 dumped many square miles of the eastern shore into the lake near what is now the Selenga River delta and still registers 2,000 shocks each year.

Lake Baikal has already suffered a very serious decline in both size and populations of omul, an endemic subspecies of Arctic whitefish that is Baikal's main commercial fish. The native creatures, specially adapted to the lake's uncommon purity, are thought to be ten times more vulnerable to habitat pollution than more widespread forms, and among the most fragile, it appears, is the minute filtering agent epishura; an estimated seven percent of epishura habitat is already lost. Other forms are being replaced by more tolerant and widespread Siberian species that usurp their age-old niches in Baikal.

Therefore it seems fatuous to assert, as the distinguished British publication *Nature* did quite recently, that "the alarms of the past few decades have been without foundation; Baikal remains more or less

On the evening of December 30, 1861, the inhabitants of the so-called Tsaganskaya Steppe heard an underground rumble that sounded like a fast approaching storm. The earth shook, the floors in the cabins rocked. Church bells rang of themselves, the doors swung open, the samovars and Christmas cakes fell off the tables. People ran out of the houses in panic and spent the whole night outdoors, while the earth continued to shift and tremble under their feet.

Things quietened down in the morning, but at noon the earth quaked again, throwing people off their feet. Cracks began to appear, grew bigger and bigger and swallowed people. The frames of wells popped out of the earth like corks out of bottles, pushed out by dirty foaming fountains.

The water of Baikal rose, gushed over the coastal ridge and swept mightily across the steppe, destroying everything in its way and inundating the whole Tsaganskaya Steppe, a territory several dozen square kilometers in size. According to official statistics, the catastrophe killed 1,300 people and 5,000 head of cattle. Whole villages with their *yurtas* and cabins were swept under water—their debris may still be seen at the bottom of the Depression. (A. Zlobin, *The Baikal Meridian*, 1960)

Babushka Bay, Pribaikalsky National Park, west shore.

25

[Epishura] constitutes 98% of all the mass of zooplankton on the north side of the lake and somewhat less on the south. In other words, epishura is the base of the pyramid at the top of which we find the unique Baikal varieties of whitefish, cod, grayling, and seal.

But epishura is not only an irreplaceable food. . . . Together with diatomic algae, it extracts about 250,000 tons of calcium per year from the waters of the rivers flowing into Baikal. Epishura is responsible for the unique purity of the Baikal water and, what is more, for its saturation with oxygen even in winter. Moreover, epishura cannot live anywhere but Baikal; it cannot survive even in pure Baikal water in a laboratory test tube. . . . (Boris Komarov, *The Destruction of Nature in the Soviet Union*, 1980)

Nineteenth-century Russian sleigh, Museum of Wooden Architecture, Irkutsk province. (Photo: Susie Crate)

in its pristine state."[2] This shortsighted assessment ignores how rapidly the lake's delicate balance is currently being destroyed. "We are nearing the point," says Dr. Galazii, "where the process of negative change becomes irreversible." Indeed, from the viewpoint of science, Baikal is already "in crisis"—unable to sustain further the effects of man.

August 22.

At Irkutsk, our group is met by Leonid Pereverzev, who in 1983 published an admiring essay on Winter's music in *Foreign Literature*. A long-time amateur of American jazz, Pereverzev is an electronics engineer who works on general theories of industrial design under the auspices of Moscow's All-Union Scientific Research Institute of Technical Aesthetics—he enunciates this cumbersome bureaucratic name with dry contempt—and serves the USSR Academy of Sciences as a member of a special task force on advanced education. A saturnine, gray-bearded man of fifty-eight with the gaunt air of some bedeviled Dostoevskian priest, Pereverzev makes no effort to disguise his bitter hatred of the Soviet system, which sacrificed, enslaved, and stunted so many million Russian lives in the seven decades that include his own lifespan. His weapon of choice is not denunciation but soft-voiced, smiling, vitriolic irony. Later I learn that it was Leonid Pereverzev who carried Aleksandr Solzhenitsyn's notes for the vast *Gulag Archipelago* while escorting the writer's wife and their three children to the airport on their way to exile.

With Pereverzev is Tatyana Khomutova of Irkutsk TV, which is making a film of Paul Winter's Baikal visit and has arranged with the state (Siberia is part of the huge Russian Republic, which is largest by far of all the Soviet republics) to provide a ship for our extended voyage. She is a native of Irkutsk, and as we drive out of the town, she

points out the concrete monstrosities erected by the state among the charming old wood buildings of her city. "Those things are our shame," says Tatyana Khomutova.

We drive up the Angara River past the Irkutsk dam that has raised the level of the lake more than a meter, turning the upper Angara into a long basin and drowning the celebrated rock just off the point where the Angara flows out of the southwest corner of the lake. (According to the Buryat people, this holy rock covered the entrance to the Kingdom of Justice.) I walk out on the point for my first good view of sacred Baikal, a soft pearly expanse of shifting distances, stretching away north, east, and south to the high Sayan Mountains on the Mongolian border, which even in late summer shine with snow.

At Listvyanka we board our ship, the 540-ton *Baikal,* black-hulled and white-cabined, 46 meters in length, 9.5 meters in beam, and three tiers of comfortable and well-lit cabins. The *Baikal* is a converted tug with a crew of eight, used formerly to tow huge rafts of logs down the lake to the Baikalsk factory. The ship is owned by the River Fleet Ministry and her captain is Aleksandr Nikolaevich Bitudsky, who has a fine big chart of Baikal on the wheelhouse wall.

We depart early in the bright afternoon and head north under the mountains of the western wall. I study this new coast from the wheelhouse roof. As the day passes, the mountains grow higher; farther north they will rise steeply to the Baikal Ridge. On this western shore, there are few roads through the high mountains, and few settlements. Thirty miles east across the lake is the delta of the Selenga River, a great breeding ground of cranes and waterfowl.

Although the lake appears sparkling clear, the Selenga River and Baikalsk together have seriously damaged all this southern part of Baikal. With the north end contaminated, too—largely from new

The firm of Sir William Armstrong, Whitworth & Co. has built upon Lake Baikal one of the most remarkable steamships in the world, to ferry the Siberian trains across the lake, and in winter to break the ice at the same time. The "Baikal" was brought out in pieces from Newcastle-on-Tyne, and put together by English engineers. . . . They lived at a little village called Listvenitchnaya, a nest of crime and robbery, crowded during the summer with innumerable caravans bringing tea from China. Every civilised person carries a revolver there, and two if he is of cautious temperament. Nobody thinks of going out after dark, and every week somebody is robbed or killed. The whole population is ex-convict or worse. . . . The very day I was there the police were looking for a man supposed to have obtained work in the yard, who was wanted for killing eight people, I was told, at one time. There are a few Cossacks at Listvenitchnaya, but they are wholly incapable, even if they have the desire, of coping with the turbulent place. It may be the best policy for the Russian Government not to hang its murderers, or keep its criminals in confinement, but to turn them loose in such places. There can be no excuse, however, for its failure to provide an adequate police force to control them, or for the preposterous tolerance which allows every man of these criminals to go about armed to the teeth. A few months before my visit they held up the mail cart from Lake Baikal to Irkutsk, shot four of its five guards, and stole its gold. (Sir Henry Norman, *All the Russias,* 1902)

Lakeshore near Listvyanka.
(Photo: Ben Simmons)

29

Lake Baikal, the father, had some 330 daughters. One could still see them, the bright mountain streams hanging from the forests of the mountains standing all around Lake Baikal with their heads in the clouds, dangling carelessly like gleaming young serpents from some tall jungle top. They were all obedient daughters and content to stay close to their father, Baikal, all, that is, except Angara. She was increasingly restless for she had heard rumors of the Yenisei, the bold, resolute warrior river in the west, all year long chasing alone through the nearby *taiga.* So, one night when Baikal was asleep, she broke out of her mountain chains, cutting a deep cleft in them as she did so, and hurled herself in the direction of the Yenisei. Her father, awakened by the noise of her flight, seized a rock and hurled it after her to stop her. But he was too late. She had gone to join the Yenisei, six hundred miles further on. But to this day the rock showed above the water where it fell in the gorge. It was called the Shaman, the priest's or holy rock, because to the Buryats it became sacred. (Laurens Van der Post, *A View of All the Russias,* 1964)

Snowdrops with the Primorskii Range behind.
(Photo: Susie Crate)

towns that have sprouted up around the construction of the Baikal–Amur railway—"the heart of Baikal" is now the central section, the widest and also the deepest part, comprising perhaps two-thirds of the surface area. This "heart of Baikal" is our destination, and the "heart of hearts," so far as I'm concerned, is the Ushkanyi Islands, four small mountain peaks out in the deeps, much frequented at this time of year by the nerpa, or Baikal seal.

This first evening, studying a map, I discover that the headwaters of the great Lena River—largest of Siberia's 53,000 rivers, and the one from which Lenin took his name—spring forth up there west of the rim, entirely separate from the Baikal watershed, though both flow north 2,000 miles to the Arctic Ocean. If the map is accurate, the Lena's two ancestral streams are not far west of the Brown Bear Coast, one of the places where Paul Winter plans to go ashore. Would it be possible, I ask, to climb up to the ridge that day and have a look?

Through Leonid Pereverzev, who gallantly performs the interpreting duties for the entire ship, Semyon Ustinov, a formidably large man, assures me sternly that it is not possible, it is too high—he points straight up—it is too far! And anyway, these maps are useless! And anyway, it is forbidden by the law! I have already been given to understand how lucky we are to see so much of Baikal, which except for a few designated points such as Listvyanka, has few visitors (throughout most of the lake, there are no villages or ports). Though stricken by a peculiar longing to gaze upon the headwaters of the great Lena, I defer to Semyon's vehemence and soon forget about it.

PART THREE

The island of Olkhon is considered sacred by the Bouriats, who believe it to be the home of an infernal deity called Begdozy, in whose keeping are the souls of the wicked. To this deity they offer innumerable sacrifices. The Mongolians also have a story about this island. They believe that it was once the home of Genghis Khan.

—Annette B. Meakin, *Ribbon of Iron*

PART THREE

August 24.

THE WEATHER clears steadily all day long, and the night brings stars. I go to sleep with the soft sound of a ship's prow on a waveless surface. Our first destination, Olkhon Island, is by far the largest island in the lake. At Khuzir, on the island's western shore, the ship is to pick up the last member of our party, V. Rasputin.

The talented but controversial Valentin Rasputin, born in 1937 in an Angara River village later flooded out by the huge hydroelectric dam at Bratsk (his best-known novel, *Farewell to Matyora,* is based on this episode—"I am one of the drowned," he says), has been friends with Semyon Ustinov since 1959, when they attended university together in Irkutsk. Even then, Ustinov tells me, Valentin Grigoreivich was appealing to local writers to help publicize the fight against the Baikalsk paper factory. Rasputin since has lent strong support to such environmental initiatives as the scrapping of a desperate plan to reverse the flow of north Siberian rivers to restore water to the vanishing Aral Sea.

Mr. Rasputin, whom I behold for the first time next morning over a breakfast of dark bread and cabbage and raw omul (the delicious fish that is the main catch of the once prosperous Baikal fishery), had fled from Irkutsk to Khuzir to escape the plague of Western environmentalists such as myself who were descending upon this threatened region.

Olkhon Island's dry microclimate creates steppe-like grasslands, similar to those of Mongolia, 250 miles (400 kilometers) to the south; west shore, adjacent to Maloye Morye.

35

I continued my explorations, and . . . visited the south shore of the island of Olkhon. It is about sixty miles in length, in some parts fifteen miles in breadth, and is separated from the north shore of the lake, called by the natives "the Little Baikal," by them considered the most sacred part of the "Holy Sea." The island is about eight miles from the north shore, excepting at its western end, where a great mass runs out into the lake for several miles and forms a magnificent entrance to the sacred sea. A little farther to the west the rocks rise to about 1200 feet, forming a stupendous object when seen from the water.

The people have a tradition in connection with this region. . . . They say that "Christ visited this part of Asia and ascended this summit, whence he looked down on all the region around. After blessing the country to the northward, he turned toward the south, and looking across the Baikal he waved his hand, exclaiming, Beyond this there is nothing." (T. W. Atkinson, *Travels in the Regions of the Upper and Lower Amoor*, 1860)

Sand dunes on the northwest shore of Olkhon Island.

The Soviet deputy proves to be a tall, shambling man of fifty-three, with hazel eyes under a round cap of dark hair and a small-nosed, round, red, worried face deeply lined by what looks like chronic psychic pain. His voice is muted, rather mild, and his manner shy. A pumpkin grin splits his face wide when he smiles, but his eyes remain shy, a little sad, as if he were not at ease among Americans due to charges of anti-Semitism that have soiled his reputation in the West.[3]

August 25.

Late in the morning, we go ashore. Olkhon is drier than the mainland, and the little town of Khuzir in its extreme bareness looks less like a taiga settlement than a sub-Arctic outpost in the tundra. A joint Russian–American archaeological expedition to Olkhon in 1975 uncovered two skeletons of Asiatic–Mongoloid stock, one of them 8,000 years old, and it is thought that the Buryat have been here since that time. In the thirteenth century, the nomadic Buryat Mongols under Genghis Khan, who was born in the rolling hills south and east of Baikal, ruled most of what is now the Soviet Union, from the Pacific west all the way to the Moscow River, but in the sixteenth century the last khan of Sibir was overthrown by the tsar's Cossacks, or frontiersmen, and in the seventeenth century the Buryat, at least, were pacified for good by the advent of Lamaist Buddhism from Tibet.

According to papers by American scholars kept in the ethnographic museum in Khuzir, the peoples who traveled across the Bering Strait to North America originated in the region of Lake Baikal (a theory made more interesting by recent findings that the Amerindians were not many different peoples, as was once assumed, but closely related groups from a single region). Similarly, the racial makeup of the Japanese changed drastically in the 500 years between 250 BC, and 250 AD, apparently because of the arrival of a new people who over-

whelmed the aboriginal Ainu and Jomon. According to blood-type studies described this year by Professor Keiichi Omoto of Tokyo University, this new people is also thought to have originated near Baikal. Baikal's proximity to the Gobi Desert of Outer Mongolia, once an abundant grassland swarming with game, supports the theory that this sacred lake was a gathering and dispersal point for Asian peoples.

In recent decades, the Buryat, like the Yakuts and Evenki, suffered forced collectivization, together with virtual annihilation of their shamans and tribal leaders, in what an Evenki writer has described as "an all-out war against our ancient way of life." An estimated 10,000 of the Buryat people perished under Stalin, and almost all their Buddhist temples were destroyed.

These days the Buryat mostly live across the lake in Trans-Baikal, in their own "autonomous" republic of Buryatia; its capital is Ulan Ude, on the Selenga River. Other indigenous peoples, the Evenki and Yakuts, have their own "autonomous" regions farther north. But "Mr. Rasputin" (as Leonid insists on calling him to avoid "Comrade") informs us that there are still about 500 Buryat on Olkhon, about a third of the sparse island population, and a few copper-colored Buryats, flat-faced and slit-eyed, may be seen here in the little town.

Climbing uphill from Khuzir, we cross the hard-cropped moor to a jutting rock that overlooks a beautiful clear crescent beach of sand, and here Paul Winter, in search of natural echoes, plays on his soprano saxophone the compositions that he calls "earth music." With Rasputin and others I listen a while, enjoying the solitary crooning call of the reed instrument to the immensities of sea and silence.

At the north end of the island in late afternoon, we climb across the moors. There are blue gentians in the grass, and dandelions, daisies, purple thistle. Wandering ahead, I find Semyon Ustinov on the cliffs,

Marble Beach, eastern tip of Ushkanyi Island, Zabaikalsky National Park.

huge and exultant. He points north toward a far dark island that resembles a beached whale—*Ushkanyi! Ushkanyi* is a Buryat word meaning "hares," so it is said; these are the seal islands of our destination. He swings his big arm in an arc toward the northwest where the mountain wall is shadowed in blue mist—*Ritti!* he cries, naming a Buryat sacred place on the Baikal–Lena Preserve where he lives—then down the cliffs to a grotto in a tower of white marble that is set off by brilliant orange lichens. *Buryat!* Where a ledge overlooks the black and depthless water—or so he seems to say in pantomime—the Buryats of old came to spear seals for meat and fur. *Nerpa!*

With the exception of a few odd bits of German, Semyon and I have no common language, only good will and a silent affinity for wilderness and wild things, but I do my best to convey to him how very beautiful I find this lake and his home country, from the blue sea and mountains all around to the bountiful asters that can be picked on these high moors by the bouquet. *Ramashka!* Semyon shouts, throwing his arms wide as if to welcome these sun-swept lavender wildflowers, and bursts into a *ramashka* song in the asters' honor.

August 26.

Under a gray northern sky, the *Baikal* rounds the northern tip of Olkhon Island to the meteorological station at Ouzour Bay, a small cove and pebble beach between rock portals. From here we travel inland on a truck bed to a lonely farmstead in high barren country inhabited by an old Buryat woman and her family.

Alexandra Argalovna Bozsueva is pure Mongol, her skin the color of dark copper filled with sun. She wears copper earrings, a blue kerchief, blue dress, boots. Talking with Valentin Rasputin, she explains her Buryat patronymic: her father had the name Argal, the word for an old male seal. Both the Buryat and Evenki peoples had seal-worship cults, since this animal provided meat and fat as well as dense warm fur. "I am of the Seal's family," she says. "In other days, children were given names of the wild animals, but now, of course, they are given Russian names." Her daughter is married to a Russian, and although Alexandra Argalovna sometimes speaks Buryatin to her grandchildren, her daughter prefers that she speak to them in Russian. She shrugs and smiles with the quiet composure of an old Inuit ("Eskimo") woman of North America, whom she much resembles.

As a young woman Alexandra Argalovna was forced to work on a collective farm, yet her people have retained such traditional practices as the burning of the dead, which allows the soul to travel swiftly to the spirit world. As she explains, a soul buried deep in the earth can never see the sun. Her own mother was buried in the earth because it was a time of drought, and had her family been suspected of having caused a forest fire, they would have been shot as "enemies of the people."

The old woman says this cheerfully, without resentment. After all, the leaders had explained to them that they had to work hard and sacrifice unceasingly to avoid war, since only the state and its heroic Red Army stood between the Buryats and the American bases that encircled them with missiles and hydrogen bombs.

Her father had instructed her not to be resentful but to accept with a good heart whatever came. Saying this, she laughs a deep and quiet laugh to show that she has lived accordingly, and means to accept life in the same spirit to the end.

Suddenly and unself-consciously, in a strong voice, Alexandra Argalovna begins singing. Her song is a peaceful chant about seeing the grains grow, and how watching one's children and grandchildren gives one the same deep feeling of the seasons—how fine life was

A pine tree and sand dunes, northwest shore of Olkhon Island.

41

Three water-babies—two boys and a little girl—came out of Lake Baikal to play upon the shore. They played until they were tired, and then fell asleep. The two witches Asuikhen and Khusukhen saw the water-babies lying asleep and tried to capture them. But the children, waking up, cried to the great lake and the mountains, "Take us, Milky Sea Mother. Take us, Inaccessible Mountain Father." Thereupon waves rose high on the lake, rushed on to the shore and almost swept the witches into the depths of Baikal. The little girl turned into a seal and disappeared in the lake. One of the boys turned into a black squirrel and hid in the mountains. The other boy was caught by the witch Khusukhen, and was given the name Ekhirit. He was called "Ekhirit-who-was-found-on-the-steep-bank," and it was said of him "His mother was a crevice on Baikal's shore, his father was the speckled burbot fish." (G. D. R. Phillips, *Dawn in Siberia: The Mongols of Lake Baikal*, 1943)

when the harvest was good and the children grew strong. When her song is finished, she says quietly, "Perhaps that is all I can sing now. In the old days we used to dance and sing, but now we have abandoned that completely. On the collective farm we had no time for it, they gave no holidays."

After a while she says, "There were sacred trees known to my parents and when my parents died, the trees died, too. Nevertheless, we still make offerings at those places, and we ask for rain or for fair weather. We believe in all living things. We have stones and trees we revere very much and we bring them offerings each month, and when we kill a sheep we make an offering, too.

"There were sacred places in the mountains where only men could go, but the shamans all died long ago, and even when I was a young girl, these sacred places were thought of as unimportant. In ancient times all life was considered sacred. Now those times are gone, nobody thinks about it any more."

Paul Winter offers to play for her and does so, standing in the yard on this gray day, as behind him a dark harrier hawk, crossing the chicken pen, causes a great squawking. Winter's soprano sax is accompanied by Glen Velez on the large, light, hand drum; he drags his nails to make it hum, rubs the stretched skin until it moans, flicking and tapping and rapping and ringing, his long fingers flying.

The old woman of the seal clan remarks quietly that hearing the drum brings back a sudden memory of "something very old" that had been lost, and Winter's reed instrument the sound of "a small wood flute my father played. I am very moved."

August 27.

The *Baikal* heads north again toward a rainbow over the Ushkanyi Islands. In late afternoon, Leonid Boriseivich Pereverzev taps at my cabin door, suggesting that we go forward to the bow and see the islands. Gazing over the water, he tells me about his grandfather, Vladimir Pereverzev, a man of the intelligentsia who became head of the railroad workers' union under the tsars, and led a railroad strike in 1905 that set off a premature revolution. Accused of treason, he escaped to Paris and did not return until 1917. "Eventually he died in bed, but his son did not." Boris Pereverzev was among those seized and executed during Stalin's purges of 1937.

Rasputin comes forward to join us in the bow. He points out Marble Island, the largest and highest of the four Ushkanyi, whose low east point reminds him of a sturgeon. A few years ago, he tells us, an Italian firm proposed a joint venture with the Soviets to mine its crystalline white limestone, but this project was stopped by Baikal's defenders.

"Six months before I was appointed to the presidential council, I'd approached Mr. Gorbachev with some proposals. I told him there were four government decrees protecting Lake Baikal and that not one had been implemented. Gorbachev promised he would put the Baikal question to the very next meeting of the Politburo, but the general situation in the country was growing more and more complicated and more urgent, made worse by all the ethnic unrest, so Baikal was not put on the agenda. Then suddenly, at the last Party congress a few weeks ago [July 1990], the Politburo lost all power to affect anything, while those in power in the Socialist Federation of Russian Republics, which had also been considering the Baikal problem, were replaced by new people, and their Baikal decrees were not put into effect. Eventually Mr. Gorbachev ordered his council to find a solution to the Baikal problem.

"Last spring, when I agreed to join the council, I had two ambitions—to protect our Russian culture [from corrupting changes] and to protect nature, especially Baikal. But in the light of our national turmoil, it seems inappropriate just now to insist on Baikal, and anyway, I may have overestimated my abilities as a politician. It's not so easy to solve problems just because one is a member of the presidential council! Up to now, in fact, I've found no way to accomplish *anything!*"

Rasputin has spoken and written with eloquence not only on Baikal but on a great many other environmental problems, Chernobyl included, but he has published no fiction since *The Fire* (1986). When I ask him if politics has disrupted his work, he nods unhappily. "It takes all my time. I don't think it's appropriate to resign right now but I think that in a year or two I shall. Sometimes I even feel that I should give up environmental work, but this, I'm afraid, will never happen"—here he smiles one of his rare smiles—"nor to you either. There are simply too many urgent problems to ignore."

In an elegant article about Lake Baikal published in 1981, he described how an Evenk "standing on the shore of Baikal as he was about to cut down a birch tree out of necessity would repent for a long time and ask the tree's forgiveness for being forced to destroy it. Nowadays we are different."[4] This custom is similar to the American Indians' custom of expressing gratitude to nature when they take a tree or deer for their own use. I ask him if he feels that the traditional values of original Siberians such as the Buryat and Evenki and Yakuts should be protected.

"If we'd paid more attention to their values in the past, we'd have none of today's problems with Baikal. It is a great loss to our society that we have severed our connection with that old sense of harmony with nature." He nods as if to himself. "For a long time, if somebody had told me that one of the designers of the Baikalsk plant had been a

Shaman Rock, west shore of Olkhon Island near Khuzir.

Buryat, I would not have believed it, and I would have been right. But today a huge hydroelectric plant is being planned for the Altai Mountains, and one of the leading proponents of this dangerous project is a native man—an example of what happens to us when our bonds to our native earth are broken. As soon as that Altai plant is built, all sorts of industry will follow, and the most beautiful region in Siberia will be ruined."

Saying this, he takes a long breath. "So perhaps our top priority is to protect the national, cultural, ethnic values of the local people in every region, because without those values, human beings will not even protect their own environment."

A few years ago, Rasputin remarked in Winter's hearing that Soviet environmental efforts were too little and too late, that "all was lost," and I ask if this is still his view today. He nods without hesitation. "I remain gloomy and sad about environmental prospects, not only in the USSR but everywhere. Almost all our country's rivers and lakes, especially in Europe, are polluted to a very high degree—by comparison, this lake is in fine condition—and even in Siberia there are regions where the water problem is truly serious. There are many groups trying to save the Aral Sea, the Volga Basin, but it's very doubtful they'll succeed. It will cost billions of rubles, and nobody has the slightest idea where that money will come from.

"To be sure, ecological consciousness is growing, but many still argue against environmental protection. For example, the cellulose plants polluting Baikal employ thousands of workers—the Baikalsk plant alone has 20,000—who naturally resist closing them down, since these workers have so little chance of finding jobs anywhere else without the retraining they're not going to get.

"So there seems little hope that humanity will recognize its own danger any time in the near future. We are like a man with his hands tied and a noose around his neck. The more desperately he struggles, the more the noose tightens. And the end is near."

The *Baikal* anchors off Marble Island about 6:00 PM, and we set off in an outboard after early supper, hoping for a late glimpse of the seals. But dark is falling before we reach Round Island. We have an inconclusive look along the rocky shore, but see no sign. Back aboard, Captain Aleksandr Nikolaevich consoles us with the toast he says is mandatory upon entering the Buryat Autonomous Republic.

The captain declares that in his ten years as a tugboat skipper, towing rafts of bound logs south to the great Baikalsk plant, he had wondered sometimes about all the talk of preserving these lake shores as reserves and parks, when the only ones permitted to enjoy them are Party officials and assorted higher-ups. It isn't like America, he says. In this country the people's parks are mostly inaccessible to the people, who can count on being shouted at and threatened by rude guards. Now, however, he understands the significance of Baikal, having had a chance for the first time to wander from the main commercial routes up and down the lake, and realizes how important it is to save these splendid islands, coves, and cliffs for Russia's future. Indeed, he feels grateful for this opportunity to see them, and is only sorry his young son is not along to see them with him.

PART FOUR

"There are not only fish in the lake," declared a Mongol, "there are spirits, each one naughtier than the other. The lord of the waters, Oulane-Khat, rules them, and when he's angry, it's no joke for the fishermen; he juggles with the boats like a sorcerer with shells."
"Foolish savage," a soldier then said to me,
"he believes in spirits! Isn't he an idiot!"
And the soldier added with conviction: "It's not a spirit,
it's a devil who is hidden at the bottom of the lake."
"Who told you?"
"The old people have seen him!"

—Paul Labbé, *Lake Baikal and The Transsiberian*, 1904

PART FOUR

August 28.

IN THE MORNING there is warm wind from the south, which brings the rain. There are many winds in Baikal, and one of the worst is the Brave Man's Wind or Barguzinski Wind, which bursts from the Barguzin River Valley, behind these high Buryatian mountains on the eastern shore. Still worse is the dread Sarma, or Black Wind, from the west, which may collide with the Barguzinski to lift up sudden waves fifteen feet high. "When the Sarma comes, the clouds descend to earth," says Semyon Ustinov.

Our captain decrees that there is too much wind and sea to take small boats across to the seal islands. According to his weather report, the storm is worsening, and so we seek shelter to the south and east, in Barguzin Bay. In steady rain, we go ashore at the barren settlement at Barguzin, where coal piles alongshore block out a small bare town of log houses with bright shutters and plastic lace and artificial flowers behind fretted windows.

In the Barguzin store there is nothing for sale but bread and snuff, and Khuzir is not much better; as one of our shore party remarks, every Russian store tends to look like a poor backcountry store in West Virginia in the thirties. As for Barguzin Bay, it is broad and unsheltered, and in late afternoon we return west over the wide part of the lake, bound for Olkhon Island and Khuzir. Crossing the wind, the

We arrived on 16 September (1735): the cold was already so intense that we had to stay in bed all day. A raging wind prevented us from hoisting the sail for several days, in spite of the pledges which our sailors made to the sacred sea; one promised bread, another Kopeks, and these pledges were made good as soon as we were able to hoist the sails. These acts of piety failed to win the favor of either Neptune or the North winds; a fierce wind got up accompanied by heavy rain. We were pushed out a league and a half, and it was with difficulty that we managed to reach a kind of harbor. The crew of those vessels which sheltered there, erected a wooden cross on the shore, and on it the higher-ranking sailors and passengers inscribed their names, their times of arrival, length of stay, and the main reasons which forced them to put into port. (J. G. Gmelin, *Voyage en Siberie*, 1767)

Near Baikalskoye, northwest shore.

51

The Common Dog Seal—or calf (but it does not have any likeness to a calf except in its voice, as Pliny observed)—is common in the Baltic Sea, the North Sea, the White Sea, the Black Sea, the Arctic and Indian Oceans, and, what is remarkable, not only in . . . Baikal . . . , or about 250 miles from the sea, linked with the Arctic Ocean at the top through the Angara and Yenisei Rivers, and at the bottom through the . . . Vitim and Lena, but also bred in the Caspian and Aral Seas, fully enclosed, and with no outlet, in abundance, the species brought there by chance in ancient times at the time of Noah's flood. In . . . Lake Baikal the species is so prolific that there is profitable hunting, even if the price is low. . . . They swim in quite large herds. But once they have gathered together at the end of the summer they withdraw in large numbers, in pairs, and the female, lying on her back, allows the male to come on top of her with the waves. They give birth at the end of the winter in the eighth month, on rocks or inaccessible river banks, losing a lot of blood. Generally speaking, there are single cubs, more rarely two, and in the early stage they are distinctly white, and covered in quite soft fur. In Autumn especially, they are so plump that, with their skins full of blubber . . . you can hardly see their face and feet. . . .

(continued on page 54)

Fisherman at Khuzir, Olkhon Island.

sturdy ship rolls to a degree rather surprising on an inland sea, causing the dishes to slide right off the table.

In mid-morning of Rasputin's final day aboard the *Baikal,* we visit Khuzir's fish-packing house, where he answers questions from the fisherfolk of the local cooperative, lined up on benches in a heavy drizzle close to rain. Behind them, in the packing house, the omul are split from gills to vent, salted in brine, and smoked to a rich golden color, after which they are packed and nailed up in wood crates for shipment. In recent years, due to overfishing, taking the much-diminished sturgeon and its caviar has been prohibited, and the delicious omul, which is said to emit a piercing cry when it is taken from the water, now represents two-thirds of the lake's commercial catch.

A century ago, Rasputin tells us, the omul rivaled beef as a source of protein for all Russia, but now too many fail to spawn in the silted streams spoiled by erosion from deforestation, and others fail to reach full size due to pollution. The main spawning stream is the Selenga, Baikal's main tributary on the east shore of the lake, but now the Selenga is polluted and the population of the precious omul so diminished that artificial breeding programs have become necessary.

"Where do you think our fish have gone?" one man demands, rousing a strong chorus of vehement voices. The booted men and babushka-ed women resemble fisherpeople the world over, dark-creased, weathered, gat-toothed, horny handed, and without illusions, ready to make the very most of an opportunity to agitate, yet brave, tenacious, open, with a ribald humor—survivors to the bone.

"They have poisoned our fish! When we split them, we find sores. . . ."

"Worms?" Rasputin asks.

"Well, no, but inflammations. On the liver."

(continued from page 52)

They are clever, and do not readily go near the hunter in the sea. But they can follow a man seen in a small boat, for a long time, as if full of wonder. In captivity they readily become used to man, and in the end they turn out as almost part of the family. I had some living at home who patiently endured fasting for more than eight weeks, without any significant decrease in fat or strength, and when dissected they still had fat the thickness of three fingers, and entrails covered with mucous. (Peter Simon Pallas, *The State in Asiatic Russia of All the Animals in the Extent of the Russian Empire and of Those Observed in Nearby Seas*, 1861)

Buryat fisherman, village of Tutai, across the channel from Olkhon Island.

54

"And what do you do with fish like that?"

"Those are the ones we eat," a woman says, to general laughter.

A man declares that patterns of fish movement are no longer what they used to be. "They are gone from where they were before, and show up where they don't belong—what has caused such a strange thing?"

"We must stop work sometimes, they are too few to process!"

"In July, the schools disappeared completely!"

"They cut our salaries. . . ."

Rasputin asks when the fish will return, and the man shrugs. "Who can say?" he says.

"Once our omul were large and fat. Now, as you see, they are so small!"

One man says quietly, "We are confused by all the changes. We don't know how to fish any more. We just go haphazardly."

"In the past, we caught nerpa [seals] in our nets. Now it is rare."

"I was told that seven or eight might be taken at one time," Rasputin says.

"Used to be. Now they seem to have learned to avoid our nets, or to escape them."

"Sometimes when we bring our nets back to the surface, we find only the fish heads and tails, so it's quite apparent that the nerpas eat them."

"Yes! Some say the nerpas are to blame for the fish going! Some say there are 100,000 now, and each nerpa eats ten pounds a day, so perhaps they'll eat up half the fish in Baikal!"

A woman scoffs. "Nerpas have always been here, yet there's always been plenty of fish!"

"Do you fishermen think there are more nerpas now?" Rasputin inquires.

"Ask the scientists, why don't you? The lake is swarming of them. All we are is fishermen!"

"What do scientists know? They contradict each other!"

"One told us that nerpas eat nothing but weeds!"

The people jeer.

A man complains that higher-ups who came here wished to be taken to shoot seals for sport, even though this was against the law. Few would guide them, for fear of being prosecuted, but the higher-ups cared nothing for the laws, which they flouted regularly.

One man cries out, "What do these higher-ups think about our future? What will they do to help us?"

Rasputin answers the man harshly, though his real anger, I think, is directed elsewhere. "No use asking what those people will do for you! Perhaps they won't help you at all until you start to do something for yourselves!"

"What about our women? It is very hard for them, working in there!"

One woman, mute, raises a finger stump in evidence.

"There are lots of problems here. Just look at the conditions!" This man turns and points at the packing shed behind him. "Our women work always in the damp, with water and salt everywhere, and not one labor-saving device!" At this, all the women shout affirmation, and their champion goes on to say that, although they were all people of the region, they are so fed up with the shrinking fishery and the rising cost of their hard lives amidst the greed and corruption of well-fed officials that they are ready to move somewhere else, take other work!

However, the others seem less sure, and look at one another, worried. "It's not so easy to leave here," one mutters.

"What should we do?" another asks us. "We were born here!"

"There is no way for us but fishing. . . ."

There is a remarkable kind of fish said to be found only in the Baikal—it is called "Golomianka" *(Comephorus baicalensis)*, and is to be found in the deepest parts of the lake very far below the surface. . . . It does not lay eggs, so say the fishermen, but gives birth to two young ones at a time.

There are also several kinds of sponge peculiar to this lake; one is of a rich green colour and contains chlorophyll. The natives use it, just as it is, to clean the copper of their samovars, while jewellers in Irkutsk use it in a dry state to polish silver. (Annette B. Meakin, *Ribbon of Iron*, 1901)

Early September, on the southeast part of the lake. (Photo: Ben Simmons)

Asked if he would stay if a joint venture with another country was developed for their fishery, a man answers gloomily that in the case of a joint venture the local fishermen are sure to be driven out.

"We'll go along with it as long as we get our pensions, but we all have rheumatic fever and none of us is going to make it. Sure, we'd be happy to have some other prospect, the choice of going somewhere. . . ."

"We'll see this place out with our own lifetimes," one woman decides quietly, as others nod, "but we would like our children to go somewhere else, to find a life in which they can be happy."

Late that afternoon, north of Khuzir, the *Baikal* circles a small fishing boat as its crew hauls a long gill net of green mesh from the gray-blue water. Two man the float line and another pair the leads—they have no winch—and the omul come in over the side not plentiful but steadily, one or two or three every few feet. Also in the net are large balls of a green algae which does not belong here. It appears to be replacing a main food source of the omul, the endemic Baikal algae *Melosira,* which has declined by about half since pollution first entered the lake.

Precisely how the lake should be protected has not yet been decided, to judge from the near absence of specific measures advanced by the experts and agencies from Europe and America now studying Baikal and offering advice, but all agree that the first step is to put a stop to the present sources of pollution, particularly the industrial combines at Baikalsk and at the Selenga River. Lumbering is now forbidden anywhere close to the lake shore, and the rafts of towed logs headed for Baikalsk, which often broke apart and sank in the severe storms, must now be carried aboard ship. Even the tourist industry, already limited by difficulty of access to the lake, will be closely controlled. All

Baklanii Island in Chivyrkusky Bay, Zabaikalsky National Park.

Omul fisherman near Yarki Island, north end of Baikal.

ships and boats that travel Lake Baikal must be equipped with devices for dealing with their own garbage and sewage, and most of the small settlements on Baikal's shore shelters have patrol boats that monitor commercial craft. However, the captain tells us that the 400 patrol boats—many times more numerous than the ships they monitor—have no anti-pollution devices, or even septic tanks. The sardonic Rasputin likens them to ambulances careening through the streets, stopping only for the people that they have run over.

In the present desperate economic straits of the Soviet Union, help for Baikal will be limited to preventive measures, in the reasonable hope that, given respite, the immense, deep lake will find a way to heal itself.

August 29.

The nearest relative of the nerpa (*Phoca siberica*) is the ringed seal (*P. hispida*), 2,000 miles to the north, in the Arctic Sea, and although the two species have been separated for at least a million years, an occasional nerpa shows vestigial spots or rings in its silvered fur.

The nerpa, which may attain a length of 4′6″ and a weight of 280 pounds, is slightly smaller than its relatives—it is the smallest pinniped on earth. Otherwise it is distinguished by very large black eyes in a flat face, strong forelimbs, and long, unsheathed foreclaws, the better to grasp fish and claw through ice, which may be three to four feet thick in winter. Hunting mostly after dark, it can swim down 600 feet and more, and remain beneath for thirty minutes in pursuit of fishes, in particular two species of sculpin and two species of the transparent oilfish called golomyanka, a pinkish, scaleless, and translucent creature with broad winglike pectoral fins which makes a daily ascent from deeper water (down to 500 feet) to the surface. The golomyanka, some ten inches long, is confined to Baikal, and its viviparous habit—

in which the female gives birth to perhaps 2,000 live young, then sinks and dies—is so efficient that its biomass—an estimated 150,000 tons—exceeds that of all the other fifty-one fish species altogether.

The nerpa prefers golomyanka to the commercially valuable omul, on which it has no important impact. Since the oilfish is fatty with vitamin-rich oil, *Phoca siberica* is fatty, too, and the fat stands it in good stead in the wintertime. The nerpa spend the winter in the water, maintaining ten to fifteen air holes in the ice. The pregnant females build lairs in the ice and have their snow-white pups in February.

The sixty to seventy thousand seals in Lake Baikal are all that remain of hundreds of thousands that were hunted to near extinction for meat, fur, and blubber, and there is still a commercial harvest of about 6,000 animals a year, which keeps their numbers at their present level. To date it has not been demonstrated that seal numbers have been reduced by lake pollution, but the nerpa is at the top of the Baikal food chain, and accumulated toxic chemicals may well have weakened its resistance to disease. In recent years there has been a general decrease in the seal population in the southern part of the lake, where pollution is greater.

August 30.

Still seeking refuge from the weather, and wishing to be close to the seal island if the weather breaks, the *Baikal* crosses the lake to Chivyrkusky Bay. This is Buryatia, where permission is needed to land, but a passing fisherman informs the captain that a large store of vodka was unloaded at Chivyrkusky only yesterday, and that the entire community, its elders and youngsters alike, drank themselves into oblivion as soon as possible. Therefore it is early afternoon before permission comes to go ashore.

In quest of solitude I climb uphill into the pine woods, which at this

A hunter one day when out shooting birds saw three beautiful swans flying toward a lake not far distant. He followed the swans, saw them come down by the water, take off their feathers, become women, and swim out from shore.

These three swans were the three daughters of Esege Malan. The hunter stole the feathers of one of the swans, and when she came from the water she could not fly away with her sisters. He caught the maiden, took her home, and made her his wife. Six children had been born to them when one day the daughter of Esege Malan distilled strong tarasun, and after her husband had drunk much she asked for her feathers, and he gave them to her. That moment she turned to a swan and flew up through the smoke-hole. One of her daughters, who was mending the tarasun still, tried to catch her and keep her from flying away, but only caught at her legs, which the girl's dirty hands made black. That is why swans, a sacred bird among the Buriats, have black legs.

The mother circled around, came back within speaking distance of her daughter, and said, "Alway [sic] at the time of the new moon you will pour out to me mare's milk and tea, and scatter red tobacco."

From this swan, the daughter of Esege Malan, came all the Trans-Baikal Buriats. (Jeremiah Curtin, *A Journey in Southern Siberia, the Mongols, Their Religion and Their Myths,* 1909)

61

time of year are carpeted with rich mosses and red and blue berries and plentiful mushrooms, white, orange, and red. I eat rose hips and sweet pine nuts from the cone. At the south end of the ridge, overlooking a Buryat camp down on the shore, is a grassy headland—a sacred place, since colorful rag offerings to old Buryat deities are tied into the trees. Off to the south is the broad isthmus with its central lake that Semyon says is the last known nesting place of the wild swan, as well as a great gathering place for cranes and other migratory birds.

Whereas only in the last decades have Russians risen to defend the lake itself, concern for Siberian wildlife has been more or less constant since early in the century. Not far to the north on this east shore lie the 650,000 acres of Baikal's first nature preserve, established under Tsar Nicholas in 1916 to protect the very valuable Barguzin sable, which was hunted to near extinction by the turn of the century. Five years later, under Lenin, protection was extended to all life on the Barguzin Preserve, plants and trees included, and today the sable, wolf, brown bear, wolverine, and other creatures have recovered. In recent years, under Gorbachev, two more preserves have been set aside, one of them Semyon's Baikal–Lena, where we will go the day after tomorrow.

By early morning, when the *Baikal* rounds the northern point of the Holy Nose peninsula on her way back out to the seal islands, the lake surface is still, smooth as pearl. Approaching the smaller islands in the ship's rowboat, the mew of gulls and ratcheting of terns can be heard over the oars at a great distance. In the channel between islands, like a black ball glinting on the pewter sea, rises the head of the first nerpa I have ever seen, and as I shout, the shining body rolls out of the water as the creature slides beneath the surface, and another head emerges, then another.

We go ashore on a beautiful beach of pale lavender marble and jade stones, then climb the bank and cross the high spine of the island to the south shore. The rocks are empty, though two nerpa surface a hundred yards offshore, and farther east, a third one, closer in, is making its way toward the rocks. Each time it submerges, we run and crouch, coming a little closer, until through binoculars I can see the languid twisting of its long hind flippers as it crosses the pale underwater boulders. Perhaps it sees us through the bright clear water, for it vanishes without coming on the shore.

I work my way around the island, hoping to catch a lone seal on the rocks, taking note of birds. A far eagle, a far falcon, a lone osprey. A flight of terns lilting along over the water turns silver against the far and dark gray mountains. I sit for a time on a rock point, eating red vaccinium berries and watching the nerpa rise to watch me, sometimes four or five round shining heads together. Soon one surfaces quite near, turning its earless mastiff's head in a slow circle, all the way around, and around again, the sun transfixed in its shining hair. In the hard morning light, the creature stares, its huge eyes like black holes in a black skull.

PART FIVE

On the summits of the bare peaks of the Lena–Vitim watershed and with a panorama of wild, grey, bare rocks before his eyes . . . the traveller feels that he is somehow stranded in a world very alien to the anthropological one, a world of lifeless, mute, wild, and grimly monotonous rocks: not only do the cries of the birds which happen by, but even the weak explosion of gunshot resound in a somehow alien manner in this silent kingdom of stone masses; not even a storm could raise a noise here, and the silent wind causes despondency, its pressure cramping one here.

—Pyotr Alekseyevich Kropotkin, *Report on the Olekma–Vitim Expedition*

PART FIVE

August 31.

THIS MORNING, on the northwest coast, Semyon announced that he and I and young Andrei Zakablukowski of the TV crew are to go ashore at once and attempt an ascent of the Baikal Ridge that towers above us. Semyon arranges with the captain to pick us up farther down the coast, and though the rendezvous is for noon tomorrow, we will take no tent or sleeping bag or even blankets. "We'll have good weather," Semyon assures us.

From the lakeshore, a forested valley climbs to a bench ridge from which a steep slope of talus rock mounts to the rim. We enter the forest of white birch, larch, and Siberian pine and begin our ascent. This is the part of the preserve called "Brown Bear Coast" or "Bear Corner" because of its robust population of brown bears, which are much larger here than in Europe, Semyon says. Almost at once we come upon signs of bear—not only feces but bear-ripped trees and saplings snapped while marking territory (to demonstrate, Semyon hurls himself into the roaring and the clawing), and even an anthill raked flat by a bear, then used as a bed by a passing red deer (*Cervus elaphus*, called izhuber).

I pick up some bear scat to see what they are eating, and Semyon hisses at me, urging me to drop it, growling a word that might be "*Triginosis!*" Semyon and Andrei speak little more English than I speak Russian, and without Leonid to translate, I climb somewhat apart, to spare all three of us the struggle of trying to include me in the conversation. However, Semyon is acquainted with the Latin names of

Banya (sauna), Ushkanyi Island, Zabaikalsky National Park.

67

In the middle of June, when the ice on the lake was breaking up and the flight of the mayflies beginning, an unusually large number of bears could be seen wandering along the shore. Their main reason for coming out of the taiga was the great swarms of mayflies that amassed near the water and served as a delicacy for them.

The bears appeared along the beach in the mornings and evenings, making rumbling noises as they headed towards the water, turning over the stones and scooping up and devouring packed cakes of goby caviar. Then, where they were not disturbed, they lounged about for hours in the water, being in no hurry to return to the mountains.

It was obvious that here the bear was emblematic of the landscape, that its outings along the lakeshore were an event as naturally regular as the flight of the mayfly and that "the bear on the shore" was one of the basic features of the primordial dense forest of this part of the coast. (O. K. Gusev, *The Brown Bear Coast*, 1986)

Harvested hay, east shore of Chivyrkusky Bay, Zabaikalsky National Park.

68

many of the plants and all the animals, and this is useful. For many years he has been a naturalist–ecologist, advising hunters about wild animals in this region. "I live everywhere here," he declares proudly.

Ravens and Eurasian jays, brown-spotted nutcrackers. In a clearing stands a small tree of orange-berried ryabina from which Andrei picks a few fine sprigs to flavor vodka. Higher up, we pass through rhododendron thicket and spiraea. We pause to eat black gooseberries, red heath berries. In sign language I inquire if the dim path we follow intermittently was made by large animals or by man, and Semyon halts, to lend weight to his answer. The only ones using this path, he informs me, banging his chest, are "*Bar!* [Bear!] *Izhuber! I!*"

Near the mountain ridge, the forest is laid open by avalanches of rough, dark gray talus. The chipmunk burunduk gives its birdy call, and there is also a small ground squirrel, gray in color. We see no other animals, and birds are scarce. On the ridge, the day is hot and humid, there are sweat bees. Semyon hurls the flow of rocks aside in an effort to uncover the trickle of water far beneath, but on the steep slope, his excavations keep collapsing, and finally he straightens up, disgusted, an ancient cross on a small chain dangling from his shirt. He is a descendant of the Old Believers, the conservative sect of Orthodox Christianity that fled European Russia when Peter the Great exposed his countrymen to dangerous liberal ideas.

Again we climb, picking our way across the talus slopes, coughing out sweat bees which keep flying into our mouths, in search of moisture. Counting on rivulets, we carry no canteens, but the day is hotter and the terrain drier than Semyon expected, and the water we find lies in a stagnant pool that elk have turned to a green wallow. Eventually there is no choice, we must descend again, losing too much hard-won altitude in the process. We travel down across rock and alder thicket

to a low wood on the saddle, where Semyon locates a shady pool used heavily by bear and other animals. ("*Bar! Izhuber! Peoples!—all trink!*" Andrei cries.) The water is clouded but not stagnant, and it is cold. We drink deeply, then make tea over a fire to go with our hard thick bread and sausage, topped off with sticky candies for dessert.

Toward four o'clock we resume our ascent, watching each step in the treacherous rock, which slides on the steep slope and could twist an ankle. Semyon hopes we will find water up there, but the rim is still so high above us, and so far, that I wonder if we can possibly make it before dark.

In late afternoon, at higher altitude, the day cools rapidly. The night is certain to be cold. Although they have dispensed with sleeping bags and water, the Siberians pack lots of heavy gear, including canned food, cameras, and a pistol. Even so, Andrei, whose archaic movie camera must weigh thirty pounds, comes jumping down over the rocks to present me with three very small wild raspberries, as Semyon berates him for rock jumping so carelessly in the loose Cossack boots that both men wear. The tart, wild taste clears my mouth of the condensed milk we have just drunk from the tin for want of water. Andrei's generous spirit, Semyon's, too, refresh my own, and I cry *Horosho!* (Good!) and imitate their thumbs-up gesture to show how splendidly I'm doing, although in fact I am thirsty and exhausted, and gloomy about the long, cold night ahead.

High up, at the base of the last ascent, Andrei finds a rivulet under the rocks, and here we leave our packs behind, anxious to get up to the rim before dark. In this last steep climb, I must stop every few feet to gasp for breath, for we have been climbing for ten hours, and the air seems thin. Step after step, with heaving chest, I drag myself, on all fours at times, toward the sky, taking pains not to look up, to avoid discouragement. *Horror show!* I cry in response to distant calls, for I

Inside a wooden yurt, the winter dwelling of early twentieth-century Buryats. Gakhani Regional Museum, Irkutsk province. (Photo: Susie Crate)

Wildflowers, Holy Nose Peninsula, east shore, Zabaikalsky National Park.

have long ago lost sight of my companions. Then I am there, in a cool wind on the rim, gazing down on the great stillness of Lake Baikal.

Semyon, huge against the sky, the sun a halo in his flaxen hair, turns and points westward, where a tableland of black rock and white lichen slopes away for a few hundred yards before falling away into a canyon deepened by night shadow. The twilight is softened by clouds of pink lavender as the sun descends like transparent fire to the sharp horizons. Already, down to the southeast, a half-moon is riding up over the rim in a stone-blue sky.

We cross the narrow Baikal Ridge, over black rock and white lichen. Semyon stamps a heavy boot on the lichen underfoot, from beneath which a clear trickle threads its way over the flat rock to join others descending to the silver glint in the dark canyons. That sinuous glint is a high mountain torrent, and there is another farther north, and these will form a confluence in the ravines not very far west of the place we stand.

"The Lena," I say, and Semyon nods, triumphant.

Scarcely a hundred yards from Baikal's rim, we are standing on the sources of the Lena, the great Mother River of Siberia. I think of how Semyon earlier said we would never be able to travel to the headwaters. In this evening silence and great solitude, broken only by a solitary hawk, those mountain torrents fading swiftly in the dark are a mysterious and moving sight. Down that river toward the north is the great salmonid, the taimen, 150 pounds or more of piscatorial splendor, which can rarely be taken, so it is said, unless it is whacked each time it leaps by shotgun salvos from the angler's confederate; down there is the Great Bend of the Lena, which some American Indians identify as the original homeland of their people.

Soon the silver glint of mountain torrents is extinguished. Deep

View from the shore of the Bay of Ayaya, northwest shore of Baikal.

down in the canyons night has come. Semyon believes (or so he will tell Leonid next day) that I am the first foreigner ever to behold these remote headwaters of the great Lena. Probably this is untrue but it's fun to think so.

September 1.

At dawn, the sun's broad golden path illuminates Baikal, but as we descend from the Baikal Ridge and the sun rises, the glitter fades to an old gold, then silver, and finally to soft pewter in the mist. In the saddle between the talus slope and the descent through forest to the lake, we surprise no deer or bear, only a mountain or varying hare, which moves off in no haste, white tail waving in the rhododendron.

Evergreen forest, a steep grassy slope, hawks, autumn wind. Asters and gentians, yellow daisies, purple vetch. The *Baikal* passes offshore in the mist, bound south for the cove where she will pick us up for the return to the Ushkanyi Islands; the helmsman does not see Semyon waving from the forest.

According to a fisherman, seals are lying out on the north end of Narrow Island. We go ashore on the south end and walk the island's length through sunny larch wood, moving in silence over the thick mosses, then crawling to the edge of the low bank.

Today, at last, we are among the nerpa, which are crowded sociably on two large boulders, spilling over onto smaller rocks along the shore. A group of about forty takes the air directly in front of us, and a second group of similar size basks on other boulders to the south. (There are no young among them, since pups of the year, born in February and March, remain in the open water during their first summer.) Those emerging from the water are a shining black, but as the silver hair tips dry, the fur turns a deeper gray color, with a silver sheen

Storm, northwest shoreline on the Brown Bear Coast.

75

on the fat rolls on the neck, until finally the whole animal is lustrous silver gray, shading to yellowish white along the belly. Once their place is secure, the animals arch their backs, twisting smooth heliotropic heads toward the sun. With one draped over the other and both hoisted off the rock, the hind flippers resemble a soft propeller.

A seal wishing to gain a place upon the boulder may lounge a long while at the water's edge, using its strong bearish forepaw to splash water into the squinched-up face of the incumbent, which may hide its own head underwater while attempting to splash water back at its tormentor. Places on the rock are sparred over more or less amicably, with little or no biting and snarling, and even the largest of the males appear to be unscarred on their heads and necks, a very unusual condition among pinnipeds. (A seal biologist from San Diego Sea World, Dr. Brent Stewart, later tells me in Irkutsk that *P. siberica* is even gentler than the equable ringed seal, permitting itself to be handled without biting when caught in nets for scientific purposes.)

The broad boulders are scarcely ten yards from the bank, and so the nerpa seem aware of an intrusion, rolling their round heads to stare, then going on about their business, which is basking. Excepting occasional predation by bears, they have no enemies apart from man, whom they don't associate with pale faces in the moss (the hunters usually come at them across the ice). Not unless we stand or thrash or otherwise act rudely will these gentle animals charge from their rock in the galumphing panic and loud water crash that alerts all others within earshot. No, they simply stare and stare, unblinking, while the eastern sun, piercing the open forest, reflects from the immense black eyes in strange gleams of ruby fire. Nostrils flare open, then shut tight, as if in anticipation of the night pursuit of the translucent golomyanka, making its evening ascent from the depths of the oldest and the deepest lake on earth.

Nerpa at Tonkii Island, Zabaikalsky National Park.

Shaman site carving, Baklanii Island,
Chivyrkusky Bay, Zabaikalsky National Park.

AFTERWORD

ON SEVERAL TRIPS to Baikal over the past few years, I have come to know the lake, and have listened to many people who live nearby and worry about its future.

Occupying a special place in the hearts and minds of Russians, this "sacred sea" is an inviolable symbol of the beauty and wildness often sacrificed in the name of industrial progress.

In the old Soviet order, few dared to argue publicly against the wisdom of the central government. However, a vocal group of activists who came forward to defend the lake against the proposed construction of the pulp plants sparked the beginning of the environmental movement in the Soviet Union. Now the political climate has changed quickly and radically and it is no longer unpopular and dangerous to want to save wild and beautiful places. In the new, emerging Russia, the means to do this are at hand.

First, Russian leaders must take a brave new step by shutting down the pulp plants or converting them to a more benign function. A second, braver step is for Russian representatives to the United Nations to nominate the Lake Baikal region for designation as a World Heritage Site.

An advisory group from UNESCO has already investigated Baikal and found that it fulfills all the criteria of "outstanding universal value" that must be met for accreditation, but it remains for the Russian government to nominate Baikal formally. Once this is done, UNESCO can step in and provide for an internationally sanctioned administrative framework to ensure a coherent system of planning, management, and mitigation of threats to Baikal. World Heritage status for Lake Baikal would not only assure the lake's integrity and purity. It could also have important benefits in the new—but struggling—Russian economy, which at this point is very vulnerable to the pressures of unbridled foreign investment and development.

Tourism, by recent estimates (found in the *Travel Industry World Handbook*), has become an enormous global industry. World tourism receipts will soon grow to $3 trillion in annual income—surpassing every other industry by billions of dollars. With World Heritage designation officially recognizing the universal importance and magnificence of Baikal, the tourists' dollars certainly would follow.

I urge you to contact the leaders of the Russian Republic and encourage them to nominate Lake Baikal as a United Nations World Heritage Site. This huge old lake—clear, beautiful, and surrounded by wildness—is a world treasure, and part of the world's heritage, but it can remain so only if the world treats it as such and comes to its rescue.

DAVID BROWER
Earth Island Institute

Ground cover, Chivyrkusky Bay, Zabaikalsky National Park.

ACKNOWLEDGMENTS

Contributors to this book would like to express their gratitude to the following: Sierra Club Books Editor David Spinner for his tact and skill in reconciling the various elements and strong opinions swirling around this project; Dave Brower for organizing the environmental expeditions and meetings on the preservation of Baikal; Fran Macy at the Center for US–USSR Initiatives for coordinating those efforts; Gary Cook, Director of Baikal Watch; George Davis; Hank and Irina Birnbaum; Grigori Galazii, champion and defender of Baikal; Boris Dmitriev; Leonid Yevseyev; Pavel Bosnin; Evgenii Scherbakov; Jenny Sutton; Sergei Pisarev; Fyodor Vetlakov; Pyotr Abramyonok and Zoya Simkina, Director and Assistant Director of Pribaikalsky National Park; Vladimir Melnikov, Director of Zabaikalsky National Park, and Evgenii Ovdin; Dr. Brent Stewart of Scripps Oceanographic Institute; Albert C. Todd, who opened the door to the Baikal Expedition; Tatyana Khomutova for making the boat trip possible; Leonid Pereversev for being the link between Russians and Americans during the many months it took to organize the voyage; Valentin Rasputin for his cooperation in arranging for the boat and for his dedication to preserving Baikal; and Kathy Cowles, Christina Andersen, Jim Butler, and Chantal Harris of Living Music; and Sarah Laird and Nick Howard for all their support of the project.

NOTES

1. "*Perestroika* vs. a Growing Wasteland," Jeff Trimble, *U.S. News and World Report* (December 5, 1988): 44–45.
2. "Baikal Centre takes Step Forward," John Maddox, *Nature* 341 (October 1989): 481.
3. "The Blue Pearl of Siberia," Peter Matthiessen, *New York Review of Books* (February 14, 1991): 37–47.
4. *Siberia on Fire,* Valentin Rasputin, De Kalb, Illinois: Northern Illinois University Press, 1989: 193.

SOURCES AND PERMISSIONS

Grateful acknowledgment is given to the following publishers and other copyright holders for their permission to use the selections reprinted in this book:

The Foreign Languages Publishing House, Moscow, for the excerpt from *The Baikal Meridian,* by A. Zlobin, translated by Ivanov-Mujiev: 1960.

Chez Liley for the translation of "Lake Baikal and the Transsiberian," by Paul Labbé in *Tour du Monde,* n.s. année 10, 1904.

William Morrow & Company, Inc., New York, and Chatto & Windus Ltd./The Hogarth Press, London, for the excerpt from *A View of All the Russias,* by Laurens van der Post: 1964.

In the village of Katun, Chivyrkusky Bay, Zabaikalsky National Park.

Northern Illinois University Press, De Kalb, Illinois, for the excerpt from "Baikal" in *Siberia on Fire,* by Valentin Rasputin, translated by Gerald Mikkelson and Margaret Winchell: 1989.

Progress Publishers, Moscow, for the excerpt from the *Report on the Olekma–Vitim Expedition,* by Pyotr Alekseyevich Kropotkin, quoted in the chapter by Sergei Bogatko and translated by David Sinclair-Loutit in *The Great Baikal–Amur Railway,* compiled by V. I. Malashenko, edited by I. Sobolev: 1977.

Grace Kennan Warnecke of the Kennan family for the excerpt from *The Siberian Exile System,* by George Kennan, reprinted by Praeger Publishers: 1970.

M. E. Sharpe, Inc., Armonk, New York 10504, for permission to reprint from *The Destruction of Nature in the Soviet Union,* by Boris Komarov, translated by Michel Vale and Joe Hollander: 1980.

Suzanne Theasby for the translation of *The State In Asiatic Russia Of All The Animals In The Extent Of The Russian Empire And Those Observed In Nearby Seas,* by Peter Simon Pallas: 1811.

Albert C. Todd for his translations of: "Baikal," by Yevgeny Yevtushenko: 1978; "From Where Does the Name 'Baikal' Come?" from the folklore recordings by L. E. Eliasov in *Baikal Legends and Traditions,* second edition, Ulan Ude, Russia: Buriatskoe knizhnoe izdatel'stvo: 1984; "The Brown Bear Coast" from *Sviashenneyi Baikal,* by O. K. Gusev, Agropromizat, Moscow: 1986.

Thanks also to the General Research Division, the New York Public Library, Astor, Lenox and Tilden Foundations, for permission to reproduce from the following: *All The Russias: Travels and Studies in Contemporary European Russia, Finland, Siberia, the Caucasus and Central Asia,* by Sir Henry Norman, originally published by Charles Scribner's Sons, New York: 1902; *Dawn in Siberia: The Mongols of Lake Baikal,* by G. D. R. Phillips, originally published by Frederick Muller, Ltd., London: 1943; *Ribbon of Iron,* by Annette Meakin, Westminster: Archibald Constable & Co., Ltd.: 1901; *Three Years' Travel from Muscovy Over Land to China,* by His Excellency E. Ysbrantes Ides, London: W. Freeman: 1706; *Travels in the Regions of the Upper and Lower Amoor,* by T. W. Atkinson, New York: Harper & Bros.: 1860; *Voyage in Siberia,* by J. G. Gmelin, Paris: 1767, translated by and used with permission of Vivienne Liley; and to the Oriental Division, the New York Public Library, Astor, Lenox and Tilden Foundations for the excerpt from *Customary Laws of the Mongol Tribes,* by V. A. Ryazanovski, China: Harbin "Artistic Printing House": 1929.

Susie Crate, Boris Dmitriev, and Ben Simmons are freelance photographers who contributed their work to this project. Crate and Dmitriev can be reached through Baikal Watch: 300 Broadway, Suite 28, San Francisco, CA 94133. Simmons can be reached through SIPA Special Features, Yurakucho Denki Bldg. 20F, 1-7-1 Yurakucho Tokyo 100.